The Knight Light

'The Knight Light'
An original concept by Jenny Jinks
© Jenny Jinks 2022

Illustrated by Antonella Fant

Published by MAVERICK ARTS PUBLISHING LTD
Studio 11, City Business Centre, 6 Brighton Road,
Horsham, West Sussex, RH13 5BB
© Maverick Arts Publishing Limited August 2022
+44 (0)1403 256941

A CIP catalogue record for this book is available at the British Library.

ISBN 978-1-84886-905-9

OXFORDSHIRE COUNTY COUNCIL	
3303748921	
Askews & Holts	06-Oct-2022
JF BEGINNER READER	

This book is rated as: Purple Band (Guided Reading)

The Knight Light

By Jenny Jinks

Illustrated by Antonella Fant

Sir Fred the Fearless was the bravest and boldest knight the kingdom had ever seen.

There was no problem too big, no enemy too scary. At the first sign of trouble, Sir Fred would jump on his horse and off he would go. He was ready for anything, and he was *always* home by bedtime.

Everybody thought Sir Fred was the bravest knight ever.

One morning, there was news of a dragon causing havoc at the far end of the kingdom.

"We need Sir Fred!" the king declared.

"Only he can rid the kingdom of this pest."

Sir Fred arrived on his trusty horse.

"Go and save our kingdom," the king ordered.

"But be careful," he added in a whisper. "That dragon sounds pretty scary."

"No problem, I'm not scared," Sir Fred replied. And off he rode, as fearless as ever.

Sir Fred arrived at the far end of the kingdom. The dragon was much bigger than Fred had ever seen before. Its wings were as big as a house. It breathed fire that was hotter than the sun.

But still Sir Fred wasn't scared. He raised his sword, held his shield high and charged towards the dragon at full speed. This would make any normal beast back away. But the dragon did not move. It didn't even blink.

Sir Fred stopped. He would not give up that easily. He tried everything he could think of.

He made himself look bigger by putting on all his layers.

He made himself look scarier by covering himself in mud and sticks.

He made himself louder by banging pots and pans.

But still the dragon refused to leave.

It thrashed around the town, knocking down buildings with its huge tail and hiccupping fire that burnt everything in its path.

Maybe Sir Fred had met his match.

"We won't get a wink of sleep with this dragon still on the loose," the villagers said.

"Sleep?" Sir Fred said, looking up and seeing the sun setting behind the mountain.

"Uh, there's nothing more I can do tonight," Sir Fred said. "Perhaps I'll come back and try again in the morning."

"No!" the people cried. "You can't leave. You must get rid of this monster. If you don't stop it, it'll destroy the whole kingdom!"

Sir Fred did not like to let people down.

"Well… okay. Maybe a few more minutes. But then I really must be going. It's getting rather late," he said. The dragon hiccupped again, sending flames shooting past his head.

"We need to put out this fire!" the villagers shouted.

"Aha!" cried Sir Fred, having a great idea. "That's it! Everyone, fetch all the water you can!"

They brought buckets and pans, hoses and watering cans.

While the villagers threw the water over the burning buildings, Fred threw it at the dragon. The fire went straight out, and the hiccups stopped. The dragon fled into the dark night.

"Hooray for Sir Fred the Fearless!" everyone shouted. But where was Sir Fred?

Then, somebody spotted a bush shaking at the edge of the town square.

They peered inside, and there was Sir Fred. He was hiding.

"I'm s-s-sorry," said Sir Fred.

"That's okay," the villagers said. "He was a huge beast. We were all scared. But he's gone now. We are all safe thanks to you."

But Sir Fred just shook his head.

"It's not the dragon that's the problem," Sir Fred said sadly. "It's the d-d-dark!"

Everybody gasped.

"Sir Fred, are you afraid of the dark?" they asked him.

Poor Sir Fred just nodded. How had nobody realised before?

They had to do something to help him.

The villagers took Sir Fred inside.

"You can stay here," they told him. "Get some rest."

Fred settled down in a bed by the fire with a mug of hot chocolate.

He began to feel much better.

But then, he started to feel embarrassed.

Sir Fred was a knight. He shouldn't be afraid.

Nobody would trust him to keep them safe anymore now that they knew his secret.

When the villagers woke up the next morning, Sir Fred was gone.

All that was left was a note.

"We must find him," the villagers said.

They searched high and low.

Finally, they found Fred leaving the kingdom, carrying all of his things with him.

"Where are you going?" they asked.

"I have to go. I can't be a knight anymore. You will all be better off without me."

"But you are Sir Fred the Fearless. You fight the fiercest beasts and keep us safe. We need you."

"But what use is a knight who's afraid of the dark?" sobbed Sir Fred.

"We don't care about that," the villagers told him. "Everybody is afraid of something."

Fred couldn't believe it. They still liked him!

Just then, some people rode up behind them on horses.

It was the king!

"My messengers tell me we have a bit of a problem," the king said, looking straight at Sir Fred. "I have come to do something about it."

Sir Fred bowed his head. He knew what was coming. He was going to lose his job.

But the king pulled out a present for Sir Fred.

"Open it," the king smiled.

Sir Fred opened the present. Inside was a shield. "This is not just any shield," the king said. "This shield has been enchanted so that it will glow brightly in the dark. Your very own night light. You can take it with you wherever you go, and you will never have to be in the dark again."

Sir Fred couldn't believe it.

"Thank you!" he said.

A night light. This was just what he needed.

From then on, Sir Fred was always ready to defend the kingdom from any enemy, day or night.

He might not be Sir Fred the Fearless anymore, but he was still the bravest knight the kingdom had ever seen.

Quiz

1. Who ordered Fred to defeat the dragon?
a) The queen
b) The king
c) The lord

2. How did Fred try to scare the dragon?
a) By making himself look smaller
b) By putting on a dragon costume
c) By covering himself in mud and sticks

3. How did Fred defeat the dragon?
a) He scared it with his shield
b) He threw water on it
c) He chased it with his sword

4. What was Fred afraid of?
a) The dragon
b) Spiders
c) The dark

5. What was special about Fred's new shield?
a) It glows in the dark
b) It is extra strong
c) It is covered in jewels

Turn over for answers

Book Bands for Guided Reading

The Institute of Education book banding system is a scale of colours that reflects the various levels of reading difficulty. The bands are assigned by taking into account the content, the language style, the layout and phonics. Word, phrase and sentence level work is also taken into consideration.

Maverick Early Readers are a bright, attractive range of books covering the pink to white bands. All of these books have been book banded for guided reading to the industry standard and edited by a leading educational consultant.

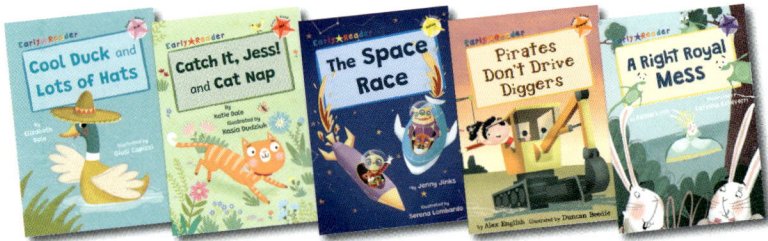

To view the whole Maverick Readers scheme, visit our website at www.maverickearlyreaders.com

Or scan the QR code above to view our scheme instantly!

Quiz Answers: 1b, 2c, 3b, 4c, 5a